THE POWER OF UNFILTERED LIVING

A Journey to Self-Discovery Through Mindful Living

Diane W. Rowe

This book is not intended to provide medical, legal, financial or any other form of advice. The content is solely for informational purposes and should not be substituted for professional advice.

TABLE OF CONTENTS

INTRODUCTION

Sarah was a young woman who had always been taught to be honest and direct. Her parents had instilled in her the value of open and unfiltered communication, and she had always been a strong believer in it.

One day, however, Sarah was faced with a difficult situation. She had been in a relationship with a man for a few months, and he had started to become increasingly critical and judgmental of her. He would often make comments about her appearance or her decisions, and it made Sarah feel uncomfortable.

She decided to confront him about it and was shocked by his response. He was completely unapologetic and unfiltered in his criticism and completely disregarded her feelings.

Sarah was taken aback and felt completely overwhelmed by the situation.

After some thought, Sarah decided that the best course of action was to set boundaries. She told her partner that she appreciated his honesty, but that she also needed him to be respectful of her feelings. She explained that she wanted to maintain a healthy relationship and that she wouldn't tolerate such behavior.

To her surprise, her partner actually listened and agreed to her terms. He apologized for his behavior, and they were able to move past the incident.

Since then, Sarah has been more mindful of how she communicates with her partner. She is more respectful of his feelings, and she is careful not to be too critical. She has also become more aware of her own feelings and how her words might affect the other person.

By learning how to deal with unfiltered communication, Sarah has been able to maintain a healthy relationship with her partner. She has learned that honest and direct communication can be beneficial, as long as it is done in a respectful manner.

Sarah is grateful that she was able to learn this lesson and is confident that she can handle any situation with the same level of maturity and understanding.

Unfiltered is a term that's becoming increasingly popular in today's world. It's a concept that promotes being honest and open about one's thoughts, feelings, and experiences, without the need to filter or censor them. Unfiltered communication allows us to connect more deeply with others and create stronger relationships. This type of communication also encourages us to live our lives more authentically and to be vulnerable with those around us. In this article, we will explore the benefits of unfiltered communication and how to incorporate it into our lives.

We will look at why unfiltered communication is important, the benefits it can bring, and practical tips on how to use it in our daily lives. We will also discuss some of the challenges of becoming more open and honest, and how to overcome them. By the end of this article, you will have a better understanding of the importance of unfiltered communication and how to implement it in your own life.

So, let's dive in and explore the power of unfiltered communication!

CHAPTER 1

The Power of Unfiltered Thought

Have you ever noticed how much power your own thoughts hold? In today's world, it can be difficult to really hone in on our unfiltered thoughts, as we are constantly being bombarded with messages from the media, our peers, and the world around us. But when we take the time to allow our unfiltered thoughts to come to the surface, it can be incredibly powerful, and even life-altering.

When we engage in unfiltered thought, we are able to tap into our inner truth and find what is truly meaningful to us. This can help us to make decisions that are based on our values, rather than outside pressures. It can also be a great way to gain clarity on difficult situations and to make sure that our decisions are in line with our values. By listening to our inner truth and allowing our unfiltered thoughts to take center stage, we can make decisions that are truly in our best interest.

Unfiltered thought can also help to open us up to new ideas and perspectives. When we take the time to really think about things without any preconceived notions or outside influences, we can explore ideas that we may not have considered before.

This can be incredibly freeing and can help us to come up with creative solutions to difficult problems.

When it comes to problem-solving, unfiltered thought can help you come up with creative solutions. It allows you to think outside the box and consider multiple perspectives. You can also use this type of thinking to process complex information and make informed decisions.

Unfiltered thought is also beneficial for innovation. When you allow yourself to think without limits or boundaries, you can generate new and innovative ideas. You can combine existing concepts or think of something completely new.

This type of thinking also allows you to break away from conventional thinking and find creative solutions.

Moreover, engaging in unfiltered thought can help us to practice self-care. Allowing ourselves to really feel our emotions and explore our innermost thoughts, can help us to develop a healthier relationship with our own thoughts and feelings. It can also help us to recognize any unhelpful thought patterns and to work on replacing them with more positive ones.

The power of unfiltered thought is immense. When we take the time to really engage in this type of thought, it can help us to make decisions that are in line with our values, open us up to new perspectives, and practice self-care. It is an incredibly powerful tool that can help us to make meaningful changes in our lives. So, why not take a few moments each day to tap into the power of unfiltered thought?

CHAPTER 2

Letting Go of Negative Thinking

Negative thinking can have a powerful and detrimental effect on our lives, leading to feelings of unhappiness, stress, and anxiety. Letting go of negative thinking is a difficult but often necessary step toward leading a healthier and more fulfilling life.

Negative thinking can take many forms, such as worrying about the future, ruminating on past experiences, and believing that bad luck will always follow.No matter the form it takes, negative thinking creates an endless cycle of self-defeating thoughts. It can limit our ability to enjoy life and keep us from reaching our goals.

The first step in letting go of negative thinking is to become aware of our own thoughts. Paying attention to our thoughts can help us identify patterns of negative thinking. Once we become aware of our own negative thoughts, we can challenge and reshape them. When a negative thought arises, take the time to consider how realistic it is. Ask yourself if there is any evidence to support this thought, or if it is based on a fear of the unknown.

Another helpful step is to replace negative thoughts with more positive and realistic ones. Think about things that make you feel good, and what you can do to improve your situation. Visualization can also be a helpful tool in replacing negative thoughts and replacing them with positive ones.

It's also important to practice self-care and to make sure to take time for yourself each day.

Spend time doing activities that bring you joy and make you feel relaxed. Connecting with nature or spending time with friends and family can also help improve our mood.

Finally, it's important to remember that no one is perfect and that it's ok to make mistakes. Everyone has their own unique journey in life and mistakes are part of the learning process. Practicing self-forgiveness and understanding that we are only human can help us let go of negative thinking and move forward.

Letting go of negative thinking is a challenging process, but it is possible. With awareness, practice, and self-care, we can become more mindful of our thoughts and start to enjoy life more.

A short story on how John let go of negative thinking.

John had been dealing with negative thinking for most of his life. He had always been a pessimist and found it difficult to let go of the thoughts that had been holding him back. He knew that if he could let go of the negative thoughts, he could open himself up to more positive experiences and a better life.

He started off by taking some time for himself. He meditated and practiced mindfulness, allowing himself to be present at the moment without judgment. He also began to focus on things that were positive in his life and what he was grateful for.

He also started to practice self-forgiveness. He began to acknowledge his mistakes and accept that he was not perfect. He stopped beating himself up for things he had done wrong and instead focused on what he could do to make things better.

John also began to take responsibility for his own happiness by making sure he was taking care of himself both mentally and physically. He began to eat healthier, exercise more and spend time with friends. He also started to get more sleep and allowed himself time to relax and recharge.

Finally, he began to challenge his negative thinking. He started to recognize when he was having negative thoughts and then look for evidence that contradicted it. He allowed himself to be open to the possibility that things could be different and that he could make his life better.

He has been able to successfully let go of his negative thinking. He no longer allows it to take control of his life and has opened himself up to more positive experiences and a better life. He is happier, healthier, and more confident. He is living his life to the fullest and is grateful for the journey he has been on.

Negative thinking can take a toll on your mental health, leading to feelings of anxiety, depression, and stress. It's important to be aware of your negative thoughts and to find ways to break the cycle of negative thinking. Here are some tips to help you deal with negative thinking:

1. Challenge Negative Thoughts: When you experience negative thoughts, it's important to challenge them. Ask yourself if the thought is realistic or if it's an exaggeration. Try to look at the

situation objectively and approach it in a positive way.

2. Practice mindfulness: mindfulness is a powerful tool for dealing with negative thinking. It involves being aware of your thoughts and feelings without judging them. By paying attention to the present moment, you can become more aware of your negative thought patterns and take steps to break them.
3. Take Time for Yourself: It's important to make time for yourself so that you can relax and reduce stress levels. Take a break from work and spend time doing something you enjoy, such as reading a book, going for a walk, or listening to music. This will help reduce the intensity of negative thoughts.

4. Talk about it: Talking to a friend, family member, or therapist can help you process your negative thoughts and gain perspective. This can also help reduce the power of negative thoughts and help you move forward.
5. Get Moving: Exercise is a great way to reduce stress and clear your mind. Even a short walk or bike ride can help to break the cycle of negative thinking.
6. Practice positive self-talk: Replace those negative thoughts with positive self-talk and affirmations.

7. Seek professional help: If negative thinking persists for a long period of time, it may be beneficial to seek help from a mental health professional.

Dealing with negative thinking can be difficult, but with the right strategies, you can overcome it. Use the tips above to help you break the cycle of negative thinking and start to feel more positive.

CHAPTER 3

Using Unfiltered Thought to Achieve Goals

Unfiltered thought is the process of allowing yourself to think without judgment, censorship, or any type of filter. This type of thought can be a powerful tool for achieving goals. By allowing yourself to think freely, you can explore new ideas, come up with innovative solutions, and create strategies to achieve your desired outcome.

One of the main benefits of unfiltered thought is that it can help you to identify and overcome any mental blocks or obstacles that stand in the way of achieving your goal. By allowing yourself to explore various thoughts and ideas, you can gain new insights into how to move forward and take effective action. It can also help to increase your self-awareness, as you become more aware of your own thoughts, emotions, and motivations.

Unfiltered thought can also help to increase your creativity. By embracing freedom of thought, you can come up with more creative ideas and solutions to problems. This can help you to come up with unique strategies for achieving your goals.

When using unfiltered thought to achieve your goals, it's important to remember that it's not about forcing yourself to think in certain ways. Instead, it's about freeing you from any mental blocks or censor ships and allowing yourself to explore the full range of thoughts that come to mind. This can help to increase your motivation and creativity, as well as help you to come up with effective strategies for achieving your goals.

Here are some ways to use unfiltered thought to achieve your goals:

1. Start with a blank slate: Remove any pre-conceived ideas or opinions from your mind before you begin. This will help you to remain open-minded and allow your thoughts to flow freely.
2. Set Aside Time to Think: When we are constantly surrounded by distractions and obligations, it can be hard to find time to just think. However, setting aside even a short amount of time each day to just think can help us access our unfiltered thoughts. We can use this time to brainstorm ideas, evaluate our progress, and come up with solutions to any issues we may be facing.

3. Ask Questions: Asking questions is a great way to access our unfiltered thoughts. Not only will it help us explore different angles and ideas, but it will also help us get to the root of any issues we may be facing. Asking ourselves questions can help us gain insight and perspective into our situation and can ultimately lead us to better solutions.
4. Make Connections: Making connections between different ideas and topics can help us come up with unique and creative solutions. This type of thinking is especially important when dealing with complex problems. By making connections between seemingly unrelated ideas, we can access our

unfiltered thoughts and come up with innovative solutions.

5. Take a Break: Sometimes, the best way to access our unfiltered thoughts is to take a break. Taking a break from our daily routine can help us gain a fresh perspective and come up with creative solutions. This can be especially helpful if we're feeling stuck and need to find a way out. Taking a break can help us clear our minds and think more clearly. Using unfiltered thought is a powerful tool for achieving our goals. By setting aside time to think, asking questions, making connections, and taking a break, we can access our unfiltered thoughts and come up with innovative solutions. We can use this type of thinking to

create a positive mindset and take our goals to the next level.

6. Reflect: Reflection is a great way to tap into our inner wisdom. By reflecting on our experiences, we can gain insight into our own thoughts and feelings and uncover new ideas and solutions. Reflection can also help us to identify any limiting beliefs or doubts that are preventing us from achieving our goals.

7. Journal: Writing down your thoughts can be a great way to express yourself without any inhibition. Use this time to write down your goals, plans, and dreams without any external interference. This can help you stay organized and motivated as you work towards achieving your goals.

Achieving goals can be a daunting task. It often requires a great deal of planning, focus, and dedication. However, it is possible to use unfiltered thoughts to help you reach your goals. Unfiltered thought is a mental process in which you suspend all judgment and evaluation of ideas and allow yourself to think freely and openly. This type of thinking can help you to generate creative solutions, generate new ideas, and gain clarity on your goals. Here are some ways to use unfiltered thought to help you reach your goals.

CHAPTER 4

Becoming More Self-Aware

Self-awareness is the ability to recognize and understand one's own feelings, behaviors, and motivations. It is a key element of emotional intelligence and has benefits such as improved decision-making, increased self-confidence, and better relationships with others. Becoming more self-aware is an important step in personal growth, and there are many strategies that can help.

Self-awareness starts with understanding your values, goals, and strengths. Take some time to reflect on your life and write down the things you value most. Consider what you want to accomplish, both short- and long-term, and what you are uniquely good at. Once you know what you stand for and what your strengths are, you can start to identify areas in which you need to work on or improve.

One of the simplest ways to become more self-aware is to practice mindful awareness. This involves taking time to pay attention to your thoughts and feelings, and to observe them objectively without judgment. This practice can help you identify patterns in your behavior and recognize how your emotions affect your decisions.

Journaling can also be a great tool for self-awareness. Note down your thoughts and feelings can help you to better understand them. You can also reflect on your experiences and use what you've learned to make better decisions in the future.

Open up to a trusted friend or counselor can also be beneficial. They can help you gain insight into yourself and provide an outside perspective. It can be especially helpful to talk to someone who knows you well and can offer an objective point of view.

Moreover, it's important to be open to feedback from others. Everyone has blind spots, so it can be helpful to ask for feedback from people around you in order to gain a better understanding of your strengths and weaknesses.

Self-awareness can also help you build healthier relationships, both with yourself and with others. Pay attention to how you communicate and the quality of your relationships. Ask yourself if you are setting healthy boundaries and speaking up for yourself when necessary. This can help you build relationships that are mutually beneficial and satisfying.

Becoming more self-aware is a journey that takes time, effort, and dedication. However, it can have powerful benefits including improved relationships, increased self-confidence, and better decision-making.

With practice and dedication, you can become more aware of yourself and your emotions and use that knowledge to create a better life for yourself.

We all have an inner voice that speaks to us throughout the day, guiding us through our choices and actions. That voice is our self-awareness. It's the same voice that tells us when we've made a mistake, when we're about to do something wrong, or when we're about to do something that might not be in our best interest. Being self-aware can be an incredibly powerful tool in our lives, allowing us to make better decisions and lead more fulfilling lives.

However, for many of us, our inner voice can be muffled by the noise of everyday life.

We become so immersed in our day-to-day tasks and obligations that we forget to take a step back and really think about our decisions and actions. This can lead to us making choices we later regret or letting important opportunities pass us by without realizing it.

That's why it's so important to take the time to become more self-aware. To help you become more self-aware, consider the following advice:

1. Take the time to reflect: Taking the time to reflect and really think about your decisions and actions can be incredibly eye-opening. It can help you understand why you do the things you do, and how your decisions and actions affect those around you.

2. Pay attention to your emotions: Our emotions can give us valuable insight into our true feelings and motivations. Paying attention to your emotions can help you understand your behavior better and make better decisions.
3. Ask for feedback: Getting feedback from those around you can be a great way to learn more about yourself. Ask them what they think of your behavior, and what they think you could do differently.

4. Practice mindfulness: Mindfulness is the practice of being present at the moment. It can help you become more aware of your thoughts, feelings, and behaviors, as well as those of the people around you.

5. Learn from your mistakes: We all make mistakes, and that's ok. But it's important to take the time to reflect on our mistakes and learn from them. This can help us become better decision-makers and more self-aware.

Becoming more self-aware can be a difficult process, but it's a beneficial one. Taking the time to really think about our decisions and actions can help us lead more fulfilling lives, and make better decisions. So take the time to become more self-aware, and you'll be glad you did.

Self-awareness is an important part of living a successful, fulfilling life. It is the ability to recognize our own thoughts, feelings, and behaviors, and understand how they are affecting our lives.

Becoming more self-aware can help us make better decisions, build healthier relationships, and improve our overall well-being.

Here are five reasons why you should become more self-aware.

1. Improve Self-Esteem: Becoming more aware of our own thoughts and feelings can help us to identify our strengths and weaknesses, and build a strong sense of self-esteem. When we know what our strengths and weaknesses are, we can work on improving them and ultimately build our self-confidence.

2. Better Decision Making: Self-awareness helps us to better understand our needs and values, which can in turn help make better decisions in all aspects of life.

By understanding our own feelings and motivations, we can better assess the situation and determine the best course of action for ourselves.

3. Healthier Relationships: When we are aware of our own thoughts and feelings, we are better able to understand and empathize with those of others. This can help us to build healthier relationships with our friends, family, and romantic partners.
4. Increased Self-Awareness: Becoming more self-aware can help us to identify and change negative thoughts and behaviors that may be holding us back. We can become aware of our triggers and learn how to better manage our emotions so that we can respond in a more productive way.

5. Increased Well-being: Being self-aware helps us to recognize our own needs and prioritize our well-being so that we can live a life that brings us joy and fulfillment. By taking the time to get to know ourselves, we can better understand our boundaries and create a lifestyle that is right for us.

Ultimately, becoming more self-aware is a powerful way to take control of our lives and create positive change. It can help us to build our confidence, make better decisions, and create healthier relationships. By taking the time to become more aware of our thoughts and feelings, we can work on improving our well-being and live a life that brings us true fulfillment.

CHAPTER 5

Challenges of Using Unfiltered Thought

The human mind is a powerful tool, but when it comes to using unfiltered thought, it can be dangerous. Unfiltered thought is when you allow your thoughts to flow without any judgment or control. This can lead to self-destructive behavior, negative outlooks, and irrational beliefs. It is important to be aware of the potential challenges of using unfiltered thought in order to better manage your mental health.

One major challenge of using unfiltered thought is that it can lead to distorted thinking. When someone allows their thoughts to run wild, they can start to make assumptions and judgments about the world around them without any evidence or facts to back it up. This can lead to paranoia and unfounded fears that can lead to unhealthy behaviors such as social anxiety and depression.

Another danger of using unfiltered thought is that it can lead to destructive behavior. This can be anything from overeating to engaging in risky activities. When we allow our thoughts to run unchecked, we are more likely to act on them without considering the consequences. This can lead to problems such as substance abuse, physical or emotional harm to ourselves or others, and even criminal behavior.

Using unfiltered thought can lead to irrational beliefs. When we allow our thoughts to run wild, we can start to believe things that are not true. This can lead to feelings of inadequacy and an inability to make rational decisions. It can also lead to feelings of shame and guilt, as well as a lack of motivation to pursue goals or make changes in our lives.

In order to manage our mental health, it is important to be aware of the potential challenges of using unfiltered thought. Taking the time to pause, reflect, and question our thoughts can help us to make better decisions and create healthier thought patterns. Learning techniques such as mindfulness and cognitive behavioral therapy can also help us to better manage our thoughts and emotions.

Unfiltered thinking can be a challenge in our lives, yet it is one that can be overcome. The key is to develop strategies to filter and manage our thoughts in a healthy and productive way. Here are some solutions to the challenge of unfiltered thinking:

1. Practice mindfulness. Mindfulness is the practice of being aware of our thoughts and feelings without judgment or reaction. It can help us to recognize when our thoughts are unproductive and help us to step back and reframe them.

2. Challenge your thoughts. When we find ourselves stuck in unhelpful thinking patterns, it can be useful to challenge our thoughts. Ask yourself if your thoughts are realistic, helpful, or true.

3. Avoid rumination. The act of concentrating on unfavorable ideas is known as ruminating. To counter this, try to focus on the present moment and your immediate surroundings.

4. Develop healthy distractions. Distractions can be helpful in breaking up chains of unhelpful thoughts. Find activities that are

calming and enjoyable, such as reading or yoga.

5. Talk to someone. Talking to a trusted friend or family member can be a great way to express our worries and find solutions to our problems.

By using these solutions, we can find ways to filter and manage our thoughts in a healthy, productive way. With practice, we can all learn to overcome the challenge of unfiltered thinking.

CHAPTER 6

Overcoming Mental Blocks

Mental blocks are a form of psychological resistance that can prevent individuals from completing tasks, reaching goals, and realizing their potential. Mental blocks can be caused by a variety of factors including fear, lack of confidence, negative self-talk, and fatigue. They can also be caused by a lack of motivation, a lack of knowledge or skills, or simply procrastination.

Fortunately, mental blocks can be overcome by taking a proactive approach. The first step is to recognize when a mental block is present. Once the block is identified, the individual can take action to address it. It is important to remember that mental blocks are not permanent and can be overcome with the right approach.

One strategy is to break down the task into smaller, more manageable parts. This allows the individual to focus on each part without feeling overwhelmed by the entire project. It also gives them the opportunity to identify any potential problems before they become bigger issues. Additionally, breaking down a task into smaller chunks can help to remove any anxiety associated with the task and make it seem less daunting.

Another strategy is to set realistic goals. This means creating a plan that is achievable and giving yourself enough time to reach your goals. Setting small, achievable goals can help to build confidence and create a sense of accomplishment.

The use of visualization techniques can also be beneficial. Picture you succeeding and completing the task at hand. Visualize what it would feel like to achieve the goal. This can provide motivation and help to eliminate any doubts or fears that may be contributing to the mental block.

Taking breaks and engaging in activities that are enjoyable and stress-relieving can be beneficial. This can help to reduce stress and provide a mental break from the task at hand.

Mental blocks can be addressed by developing a proactive approach that includes challenging negative thoughts, breaking down tasks into smaller chunks, rewarding progress, and seeking out support. With the right approach, individuals can overcome mental blocks and reach their goals.

Mental blocks can be difficult to overcome, but there are a few strategies that can help you move past them.

1. Identify the Source of the Block: Analyze the reasons behind your mental block. Is it due to a lack of motivation or an inability to focus? Once you know the source of the block, you can start to address it.
2. Break it Down: Break down the task into smaller chunks and focus on one piece at a time. This can help you overcome the feeling of overwhelm that comes with a large task.
3. Keep a Positive Attitude: A positive attitude can help you stay motivated and keep you from giving up. Remind yourself that it's possible to overcome the block and that you can do it.

4. Take Breaks: Take frequent breaks and get away from the task. Doing something that you enjoy, like going for a walk or reading a book, can help you refocus and come back to the task with a fresh perspective.
5. Seek Help: If you are still having difficulty overcoming the mental block, seek help from a professional. A therapist can help you identify the source of the block and give you strategies to help you move past it.
6. Change Your Environment: Changing your environment can help to break up the monotony and give you a different perspective on your work. Taking a break in a different environment can help to spark creativity and reduce mental blocks.

7. Try Something New: Trying something new can help to stimulate your creativity. Try a new type of exercise, a new hobby, or even just a different type of food.
8. Get Enough Sleep: Make sure you're getting enough sleep so that your mind and body are well-rested. A lack of sleep can make it harder to focus and can increase stress levels.

By following these strategies, you can start to overcome your mental blocks and get back on track.

Conclusion

Unfiltered living is a powerful way of life that can help us break free from the confines of expectations and societal pressures. It gives us the freedom to explore our passions and live life on our own terms. Through unfiltered living, we can find our authentic selves and create a life that is meaningful and fulfilling. So let's embrace the power of unfiltered living and make it our mission to live our lives to the fullest!

The book covers a wide range of strategies and approaches on the power of unfiltered thought, letting

go of negative thinking, using unfiltered thought to achieve goals, the challenge of using unfiltered thought, and overcoming the metal block. One of the key themes of the book is the power of unfiltered thought, which enlighten you on how important it is to think unfiltered. This book will help you to break that chain and make you a free person and guide you through on a new journey of life and let you live the joyful life you want for yourself.

www.ingramcontent.com/pod-product-compliance
Lightning Source LLC
LaVergne TN
LVHW052104160826
845678LV00015B/3351

9798375295183